THE SCIENCE OF A SINKHOLE

ROBIN KOONTZ

Published in the United States of America
by Cherry Lake Publishing
Ann Arbor, Michigan
www.cherrylakepublishing.com

Consultants: Stephen A. Nelson, Associate Professor of Earth and Environmental Sciences, Tulane University;
Marla Conn, ReadAbility, Inc.
Editorial direction: Red Line Editorial
Book production: Design Lab
Book design: Sleeping Bear Press

Photo Credits: Str/AP Images, cover, 1; Pat Sullivan/AP Images, 5; Hai Ou/Imaginechina/AP Images, 6; Ulises
Rodriguez/EPA/Corbis, 8; Rudolf Tepfenhart/Shutterstock Images, 11; iStockphoto, 16, 18, 28; Tomas Sereda/
iStockphoto, 21; Marshall Gorby/The Dayton Daily News/AP Images, 23; Danielle Moore/Chattanooga Times Free
Press/AP Images, 25; Michael Noble Jr./AP Images, 27

Library of Congress Cataloging-in-Publication Data
 Koontz, Robin Michal, author.
   The science of a sinkhole / by Robin Koontz.
     pages cm. — (Disaster science. Set 2)
   Audience: Grades 4 to 6
   Includes bibliographical references and index.
     ISBN 978-1-63362-481-8 (hardcover : alk. paper) — ISBN 978-1-63362-497-9 (pbk. : alk. paper) --
ISBN 978-1-63362-529-7 (hosted ebook) — ISBN 978-1-63362-513-6 (pdf ebook)
   1. Sinkholes—Juvenile literature. I. Title.

  GB609.2.K66 2015
  551.44'7—dc23   2015005518

Cherry Lake Publishing would like to acknowledge the work of
the Partnership for 21st Century Skills. Please visit *www.p21.org*
for more information.

Printed in the United States of America
Corporate Graphics
June 2015

ABOUT THE AUTHOR

Robin Koontz is the author, illustrator, and designer of a variety of books, blogs, and articles for
children and young adults. Her 2011 science book, *Leaps and Creeps: How Animals Move to Survive*,
was an Animal Behavior Society Outstanding Children's Book Award Finalist. Raised in Maryland
and Alabama, Koontz now lives with her husband in western Oregon.

TABLE OF CONTENTS

CHAPTER 1
GIANT HOLES IN THE GROUND 4

CHAPTER 2
HOW DO SINKHOLES FORM? 10

CHAPTER 3
NATURAL CAUSES OF SINKHOLES 14

CHAPTER 4
HUMAN-CAUSED SINKHOLES 20

CHAPTER 5
PREPARING FOR SINKHOLES 24

TOP FIVE WORST SINKHOLES 30

LEARN MORE 31

GLOSSARY 32

INDEX 32

GIANT HOLES IN THE GROUND

It was the morning of May 7, 2008, in Daisetta, Texas. Workers noticed large cracks in the ground near the center of town. Some residents felt the earth begin to shake. Suddenly, part of the ground collapsed, creating a sinkhole.

A sinkhole is a hole or **depression** in the ground. Some sinkholes form suddenly and grow rapidly. At first, the Daisetta sinkhole was 20 feet (6 m) across. But as the hours passed, it became much larger. Objects in its path began to fall into the growing pit. People began

The sinkhole in Daisetta, Texas, swallowed trees, telephone poles, and vehicles.

to worry that their homes would sink. Town authorities arrived to observe the situation.

By the next day, the sinkhole had grown to 900 feet (275 m) across and 260 feet (80 m) deep. It was wider than three football fields. There was little that experts could do to stop it. They could only hope the sinkhole would stop growing.

Eventually, it did. The sinkhole was one of the largest in American history, but it stopped growing before it destroyed any houses. Experts began to study the hole to identify what caused it.

Sinkholes happen all over the world. Some have devastating effects. In 2010, a three-story building fell into a sinkhole in the country of Guatemala. In 2013, a man in Florida died in a sinkhole. Jeff Bush was asleep in his bed when a giant hole opened up under his bedroom. Bush fell into the hole, along with everything else in his room. His body was never found. Local

In August 2014, a sinkhole in China swallowed a truck.

LOCATIONS OF SINKHOLES

Sinkholes occur more often in some regions than in others. In the United States, some southern states are especially prone to sinkholes. The most destructive sinkholes have occurred in these states: Texas, Florida, Pennsylvania, Missouri, Kentucky, Alabama, and Tennessee.

emergency workers waited for the sinkhole to stop growing. Afterward, they tore down the house and filled the hole. It was no longer safe to live there.

These holes in the ground have appeared throughout history, often with no warning. Sinkholes can swallow people, vehicles, and trees. They can grow large enough to devour entire buildings. Some sinkholes stop growing within a few hours. Others may continue to grow for weeks or even months.

The sinkhole in Daisetta, Texas, occurred near a salt dome. Salt domes are large underground piles or columns made of salt. They occur naturally, and they are often found near oil or gas deposits. Mining or **erosion** can damage the domes. Scientists think the Daisetta salt dome collapsed, creating the hole on the surface.

Not all sinkholes occur near salt domes. Many other environmental factors can help cause these disasters. Scientists are still learning about sinkholes. They are attempting to find ways of predicting and preventing them.

A sinkhole in Guatemala City, Guatemala, swallowed several homes.

GEOLOGIC MAPPING

Science helps us better understand sinkholes and where they are likely to occur. People can then make more informed decisions about how and where to build structures. Scientists at the US Geological Survey (USGS) are creating geologic maps of the United States. These detailed maps identify areas that are prone to sinkholes. The scientists hope to identify hazards before they become disasters. The USGS has been developing maps for more than 100 years, but recent technologies have helped improve the maps. **Geologists** use satellite navigation systems to locate land features. Digital photography helps them analyze the features.

The National Geologic Map Database provides geologic maps for almost the entire United States. USGS geologists have also developed other resources. Geologists use field notebooks to record their observations, including sketches and measurements of land and water features in areas where sinkholes occur. In recent years, geologists have used digital tools to share these observations with the public.

How Do Sinkholes Form?

Sinkholes can form in different ways, but most sinkholes form in a certain kind of bedrock. This is the rock under the layers of soil on the ground. Natural sinkholes happen in places where the bedrock is soluble, meaning that it can easily dissolve in water. Salt, gypsum, dolomite, and limestone are all types of soluble bedrock.

When rain falls, the water absorbs carbon dioxide from the air. Over time, rainwater seeps through the soil. The combination of water and carbon dioxide

Sinkholes occur in areas with soluble bedrock, such as limestone.

forms a weak acid that can create holes in bedrock. The soluble rock then soaks up water like a sponge.

Scientists recognize three main types of sinkholes. If the soluble rock is close to the surface, rainwater may begin to dissolve the bedrock and spread through cracks. The acidic water seeps underground, creating more holes. The water also carries away dissolved rock on the surface. This kind of sinkhole is called a dissolution sinkhole.

A cover-subsidence sinkhole happens when the soluble rock is below layers of soil or loose **sediment**.

Rainwater dissolves the soluble rock, creating holes. The sandy sediments from above fill in the holes. Over time, the ground sinks very slowly, as if it is deflating.

Some dissolution sinkholes and cover-subsidence sinkholes develop over hundreds of years. Cover-collapse sinkholes develop much more quickly. They form in places with clay sediment at the surface. In these places,

COVER-COLLAPSE SINKHOLE

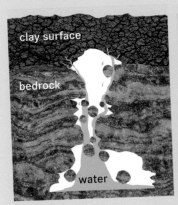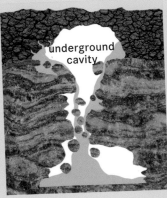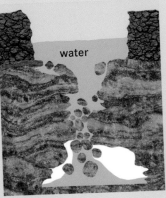

clay surface

bedrock

water

underground cavity

water

In places with mostly clay surfaces, underground holes may form in soluble bedrock. Sinkholes happen when the surfaces collapse.

[21ST CENTURY SKILLS LIBRARY]

SINKHOLES IN YUCATÁN

Yucatán, Mexico, has so much soluble limestone that there are few rivers and lakes on the surface. Rainwater seeps into the bedrock, creating underground caves. The area has many cover-collapse sinkholes, some of them hundreds of feet deep. These sinkholes are commonly known as cenotes. The ancient Maya relied on these cenotes for drinking water. People still use water from them today.

underground caves or cavities form while the surface remains stable. Floods and other forces can weaken the clay surface. If an underground **cavity** grows upward, the surface may eventually collapse. In just a few hours, cover-collapse sinkholes can spread rapidly, swallowing everything in the way.

Some sinkholes have natural causes, such as heavy rainfall. Others result from human activity. In areas where people live, all sinkholes can be disastrous.

CHAPTER 3

NATURAL CAUSES OF SINKHOLES

Either too much water or too little water can trigger a sinkhole. As groundwater seeps through the soil, it collects beneath the surface. The **water table** is the highest point of the ground that is completely saturated, or filled, with water. Sudden changes in the water table often cause sinkholes.

Heavy rain or flooding can cause the water table to rise. As more water seeps underground, the bedrock dissolves more quickly. Soluble rock and soil are carried away in the rush of water. The erosion and water pressure can cause underground caverns to collapse, forming a sinkhole.

Disappearing water also creates sinkholes. A **drought** can cause the water table to drop. Water supports underground caverns. If the water table drops, part of the cavern structure goes away. The cavern roof might collapse, bringing down everything above it.

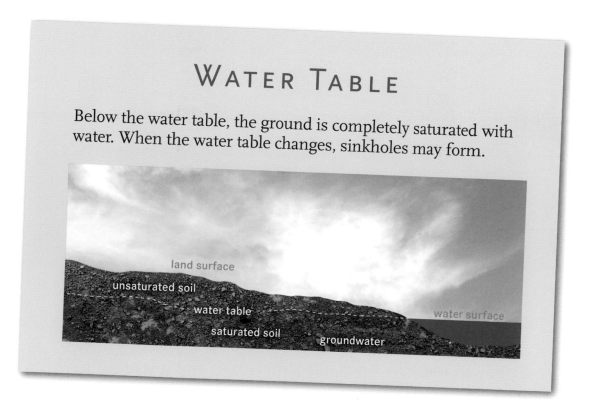

WATER TABLE

Below the water table, the ground is completely saturated with water. When the water table changes, sinkholes may form.

land surface

unsaturated soil

water table

water surface

saturated soil

groundwater

A sinkhole formed an underground cavern in Wayne County, Tennessee.

Most people living in Florida get their water from **aquifers** in the limestone. They drill below a water table to pump the water out. The aquifers help support soil on the surface. Changes in aquifer water levels due to drought, flooding, or human activity can cause soil to collapse into the underground cavity.

Where did all the limestone in Florida come from? More than a hundred million years ago, the peninsula of Florida was beneath the ocean. **Mollusks** and certain kinds of algae lived in the shallow areas. As the water receded over time, their remains dried into limestone. Massive limestone reefs formed over the landscape. In time, the water channel closed between Florida and the rest of North America. Sand and clay slowly covered the

BENEFITS OF SINKHOLES

Sinkholes filled with sand, clay, and water can spread into large wetlands and water channels. Many natural lakes in Florida began as sinkholes. Later, they were plugged by sediment and debris. Ancient sinkholes are believed to be the origins of the Florida Everglades. These expansive swamps are home to plants, trees, insects, birds, amphibians, and fish.

reefs, turning the entire region into layers of sand, clay, and limestone. The ancient reefs are now underneath Florida.

In recent years, people have reported more sinkholes than ever, in Florida and in other places around the world. That is partly because houses, highways, and even entire cities are being built over **karst** terrain. As a result, both natural and human-caused sinkholes form.

Cherokee Sink, a lake in Florida, formed when a sinkhole filled with rainwater.

ANCIENT SINKHOLE

Since 1977, underwater archaeologists have been exploring Little Salt Spring, an ancient Florida sinkhole. They have found weapons and bones that are approximately 12,000 years old. In one discovery, scientists found the remains of an extinct giant land tortoise. They also found tools from some of the earliest North Americans. These objects were in water that was mostly free of bacteria. As a result, the objects were well preserved.

The scientists believe that hunters caught their prey in the area. They may have used the sinkhole as a trap. The sinkhole was likely also a popular place to get fresh water. The ancient sinkhole has proven to be home to some of the earliest evidence of humans in the Western Hemisphere. The remains that were found belonged to people who lived among woolly mammoths and giant ground sloths, up to 12,000 years ago.

CHAPTER 4

HUMAN-CAUSED SINKHOLES

Not all sinkholes are natural. Humans are responsible for some of the most devastating sinkholes around the world. Many human-caused sinkholes occur in crowded areas, such as cities.

For many years, people have mined or drilled for oil, gas, and coal. Some sinkholes form above old or abandoned mine shafts. Building in fragile karst terrain can also trigger the formation of sinkholes.

Blocking or changing the natural flow of water can cause the ground to collapse. When people build a road

Sinkholes may form on top of old mine shafts.

or parking lot in a grassy area, they affect where rainwater can go. The water usually seeps into the soil throughout a grassy area. But on highways or parking lots, the water runs off. More water soaks into the ground at a single point. This can create sinkholes.

Leaking waterlines that are not repaired can cause erosion. Underground water pipes can burst from age or faulty construction. The leaking water eats away at the surrounding soil, and a sinkhole can form. Storm drainpipes under the ground might break during heavy rains. Rainwater can surge into the soil underneath roadways and structures. The damaged **infrastructure** can collapse into massive sinkholes.

Underground transit networks, such as trains and subways, can also cause sinkholes. These sinkholes usually occur during construction. But some also occur long after the networks are built. Some cities and towns have abandoned underground structures such as wells, oil tanks, and septic systems. These decaying systems can suddenly collapse, causing sinkholes.

Humans cause some sinkholes, but they can also help prevent them. People can avoid building in areas that are especially prone to sinkholes. Cities and towns can fix underground leaks and broken infrastructure. These efforts may decrease the number of sinkholes. However, it is still unclear whether natural sinkholes can be prevented or even predicted. There are many things about sinkholes that scientists still do not know.

Leaking water pipes in Iowa caused a sinkhole to form in 2014.

CHAPTER 5

PREPARING FOR SINKHOLES

Sinkholes occur all over the world, wherever there is soluble bedrock. They can cause damages that cost millions of dollars to repair. Sinkholes can harm water resources and make entire communities unlivable. In recent years, geologists have been using special equipment to track areas where sinkholes may form.

Geologists use radar to locate underground caverns. **Seismic** equipment tells them about movements beneath Earth's surface. Soil survey reports measure the amount of soluble bedrock in an area. This information helps scientists locate where cracks and cavities are forming. Geologists and engineers know that sudden changes in the groundwater might increase the size of these cracks.

People sometimes develop communities in areas with unstable terrain. Geologists and engineers make these areas safer for development. They install drainage systems and add rock, concrete, or gravel. Knowing

Workers study the area near a sinkhole on a highway in Tennessee.

more about areas prone to sinkholes helps builders and local governments make decisions about land use.

Sometimes there are signs that a sinkhole is forming. Fresh cracks in a house or building foundation might be a sign that the area is sinking. A cracked sidewalk or roadway may warn of a future collapse. The cracks might be places where water is flowing into a cave deep underground. If a tree suddenly leans, a sinkhole might be forming underneath its root system. Experts should investigate these signs.

THE CORVETTE MUSEUM SINKHOLE

In 2014, a large sinkhole opened up under the Corvette Museum in western Kentucky. This museum exhibits Corvette sports cars. The sinkhole was 60 feet (18 m) deep. It swallowed eight rare and valuable cars. People knew caves were in the area, but no one knew a cavern existed directly below the museum. It most likely collapsed because groundwater dissolved the underground limestone.

*A sinkhole underneath the Corvette Museum
in Kentucky swallowed eight cars.*

Fortunately, most sinkholes do not cause destruction or death. If a sinkhole is left alone, soil often eventually plugs it up. Then it stores water as a pond or lake, providing a natural resource for wildlife. A sinkhole can also become an entrance to a cave system below. Sometimes a sinkhole reveals a large underground cavern that explorers have never seen before.

In areas where people live, sinkholes still pose dangers. Scientists can identify areas that are at risk for sinkholes. But they cannot reliably predict when and

A geologist explores underground caves.

where the sinkholes will appear. Some researchers are working to change that. Scientists with the National Aeronautics and Space Administration have radar technology that may someday map out areas where sinkholes are likely to form. Geologists are experimenting with ways to monitor water levels and other factors. Soon they may be able to prevent destruction from sinkholes.

Predicting Sinkholes

Engineer Boo Hyun Nam is trying to find ways to predict sinkholes before they form. Nam put together a team of geologists, soil chemists, and engineers. These experts are monitoring areas where natural sinkholes might occur. Nam and his team want to identify signs that appear before a sinkhole forms. They plan to develop a warning system that could give people time to escape.

The team studied a database of known sinkholes. They looked for patterns to predict the most likely areas for a sinkhole. They decided that groundwater levels were a possible way to predict where sinkholes could form. Researchers created a model of a sinkhole inside an oil drum. They added pipes and sensors to monitor the water levels and temperature of the soil. The team then added water to imitate rain. They watched as a miniature sinkhole formed. The team's experiments showed possible connections between groundwater levels and sinkholes.

Top Five
Worst Sinkholes

1. **Berezniki, Russia, 2007**
   Sinkholes are common in Berezniki, due to flaws in an underground mine. The largest sinkhole is more than 780 feet (238 m) deep. This sinkhole destroyed a warehouse. Authorities evacuated thousands of residents to avoid injuries or deaths.

2. **Assumption Parish, Louisiana, 2012**
   A manmade salt cavern suddenly collapsed, creating a sinkhole about the size of a football field. The growing toxic sinkhole contains explosive methane gas and is still causing local earthquakes.

3. **Winter Park, Florida, 1981**
   A barking dog alerted people to this sinkhole, which began in her owner's yard. The sinkhole swallowed a two-story house, a car dealership, and at least five cars.

4. **Guatemala City, Guatemala, 2010**
   During a tropical storm, heavy rainfall caused a large sinkhole to open up in downtown Guatemala City. Several buildings fell into the sinkhole. It was approximately 60 feet (18 m) wide and 300 feet (91 m) deep.

5. **Daisetta, Texas, 2008**
   On May 7, 2008, the collapse of a salt dome created a large sinkhole in Daisetta, Texas. By the next day, it had expanded to 900 feet (275 m) wide. It was 260 feet (80 m) deep.

LEARN MORE

FURTHER READING

Clifford, Tim. *Let's Explore Science: Geology*. Vero Beach, FL: Rourke Publishing, 2009.

Kopp, Megan. *Earth Science: Sinkholes*. New York: Weigl Av2, 2013.

Price, Jane. *Underworld: Exploring the Secret World Beneath Your Feet*. Toronto: Kids Can Press, 2014.

WEB SITES

Oregon Museum of Science and Industry: Build a Sinkhole
www.omsi.edu/sites/all/FTP/files/expeditionnw/5.E.1.Hole.pdf
This Web site provides lessons and activities about physical aspects of sinkholes.

PBS Kids: Sinkholes
pbskids.org/dragonflytv/show/sinkholes.html
This Web site provides details about how sinkholes form and instructions for making a model sinkhole.

GLOSSARY

aquifers (AH-kwi-ferz) beds of sand, rock, or gravel that can hold water

cavity (KA-vit-ee) a hole or hollow space

depression (dee-PREH-shun) a sunken area in the ground

drought (DROWT) a long spell of very dry weather

erosion (ee-ROW-zhun) the process in which wind, water, and other factors wear away Earth's surface

geologists (DJEE-ah-low-jists) scientists who study nature and the history of Earth

infrastructure (IN-fru-struhk-chur) structures and equipment, such as roads and bridges, needed for a city or town to function

karst (KARST) soluble bedrock that has eroded, producing cracks, sinkholes, and caverns

mollusks (MOL-uhsks) animals with soft bodies and no spines, usually covered by shells

sediment (SED-ih-ment) rocks, sand, or dirt that has been carried to a place by water, wind, or a glacier

seismic (SIZE-mihk) related to vibrations or tremors under Earth's surface

water table (WA-tur TAY-bul) the highest point underground where fractures in the bedrock are completely saturated with water

INDEX

caves, 13, 15, 16, 24, 26, 27, 28
cover-collapse sinkholes, 12–13
cover-subsidence sinkholes, 11–12

Daisetta, Texas, 4–5, 7–8, 30
dissolution sinkholes, 11

erosion, 8, 14, 21, 22

Florida, 6–7, 16–19, 30

geologists, 9, 24–25, 28, 29
Guatemala, 6, 8, 22, 30

human-caused sinkholes, 13, 20–23

karst, 18, 20

lakes, 13, 17, 18, 27

limestone, 10, 11, 13, 16–18, 26

salt domes, 7–8, 30
sediment, 11, 12, 17
sinkhole formation, 10–13, 15, 20–21, 26, 27–28
sinkhole prediction, 8, 23, 27–28, 29
sinkhole preparation, 23, 24–29